GRAPHIC LIBRARY®

GRAPHIC SCIENCE

UNDERSTANDING GLOBAL WARMING

WITH MAX AXIOM SUPER SCIENTIST

Agnieszka Biskup

illustrated by Cynthia Martin and Bill Anderson

Raintree

www.raintreepublishers.co.uk
Visit our website to find out
more information about
Raintree books.

To order:
☎ Phone +44 (0) 1865 888066
🖨 Fax +44 (0) 1865 314091
💻 Visit www.raintreepublishers.co.uk

Raintree is an imprint of Capstone Global Library Limited, a company incorporated in England and
Wales having its registered office at 7 Pilgrim Street, London EC4V 6LB
Registered company number: 6695882

"Raintree" is a registered trademark of Pearson Education Limited, under licence to Capstone Global
Library Limited

Text © Capstone Press 2008
First published by Capstone Press in 2008
First published in hardback in the United Kingdom by Capstone Global Library in 2010
The moral rights of the proprietor have been asserted.

N 978 1 4062 1462 8 (hardback)
14 13 12 11 10

ibrary Cataloguing in Publication Data
Biskup, Agnieszka.
bal warming. -- (Graphic science)
363.7'3874-dc22
d for this book is available from the British Library.

Art Director and Designer: Bob Lentz and Thomas Emery
Cover Artist: Tod Smith
Colourist: Krista Ward
UK Editor: Diyan Leake
UK Production: Alison Parsons
Originated by Capstone Global Library
Printed and bound in China by South China Printing Company Limited

Acknowledgements
The publisher would like to thank the following for permission to reproduce copyright material:
NASA p. 15; Shutterstock p. 21 (Margaud)

ROEC

12/10

2 5 JAN 2011

1 8 MAR 2013

This book should be returned/renewed by the latest date shown above. Overdue items incur charges which prevent self-service renewals. Please contact the library.

Wandsworth Libraries
24 hour Renewal Hotline

CONTENTS

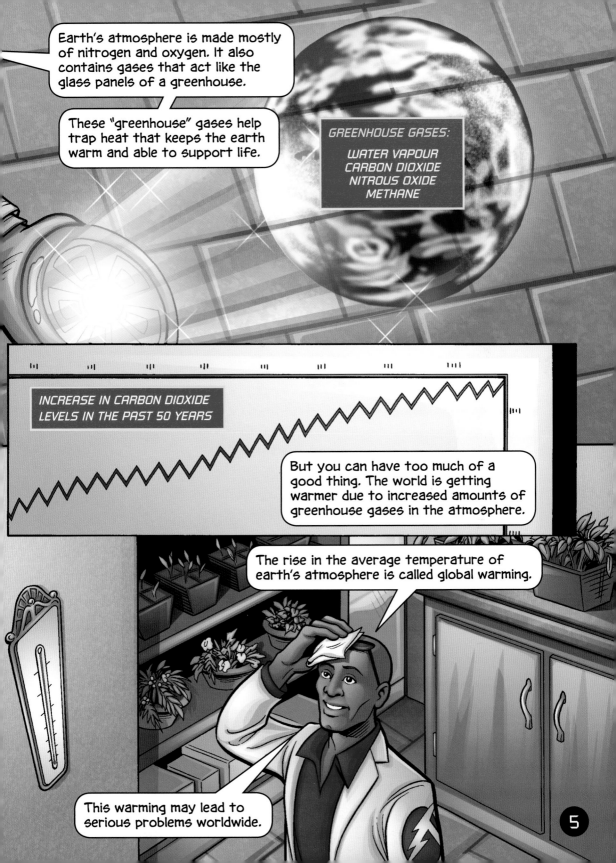

Let's take a closer look at how the greenhouse effect works.

Our atmosphere allows the sun's rays to warm the earth's surface.

Heat from the earth is then radiated out into space.

SUNLIGHT

RADIATED HEAT

RADIATED HEAT

But some heat is also absorbed by greenhouse gases and radiated back to earth. Without the greenhouse effect, the earth would be too cold for most forms of life.

HOT AND COLD MOON

The moon has no atmosphere. Its equator is a blistering 127 degrees Celsius (260 degrees Fahrenheit) in daylight. In darkness the temperature drops to a frigid minus 173 degrees Celsius (minus 280 degrees Fahrenheit).

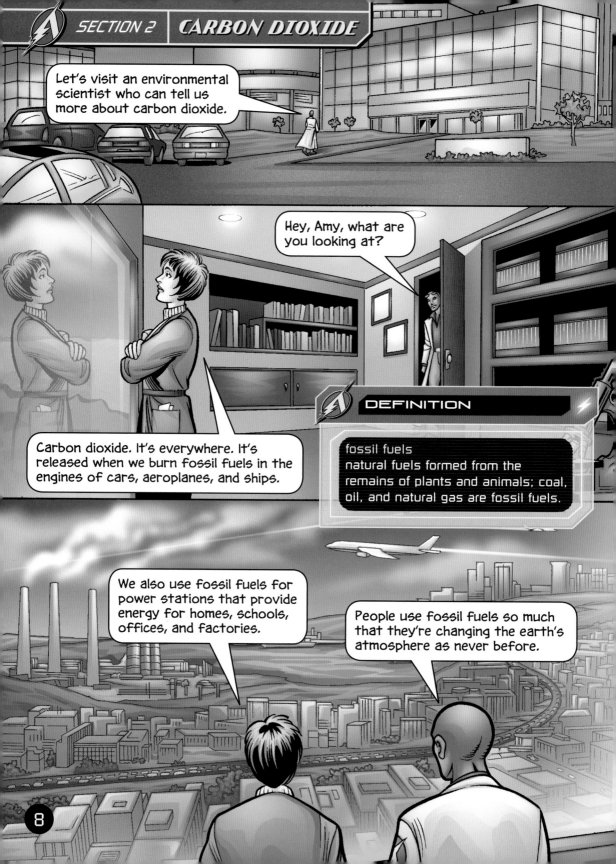

Let's visit an environmental scientist who can tell us more about carbon dioxide.

Hey, Amy, what are you looking at?

Carbon dioxide. It's everywhere. It's released when we burn fossil fuels in the engines of cars, aeroplanes, and ships.

DEFINITION

fossil fuels
natural fuels formed from the remains of plants and animals; coal, oil, and natural gas are fossil fuels.

We also use fossil fuels for power stations that provide energy for homes, schools, offices, and factories.

People use fossil fuels so much that they're changing the earth's atmosphere as never before.

Trees, plants, and even the oceans help take up extra carbon dioxide from the atmosphere.

But in many places, such as the rainforests of South America, people are clearing the forests for farmland.

DEFINITION

deforestation
the clearing of forests by cutting or burning trees

Trees that are burned or left to decompose release carbon dioxide into the air.

Because these dead trees no longer take in carbon dioxide, the build-up of greenhouse gases increases.

DRY CLIMATE

Climate describes the average weather of a certain area over many years.

TROPICAL CLIMATE

TEMPERATE CLIMATE

POLAR CLIMATE

Florida in the US, for example, is normally warm and humid.

And Antarctica is cold and dry.

Climates change over time, but global warming is changing them faster than normal.

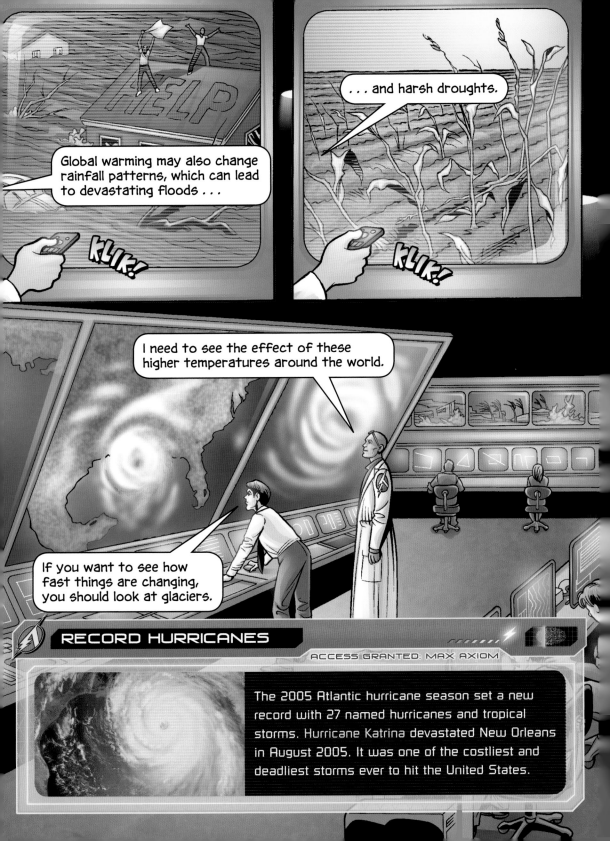

Global warming may also change rainfall patterns, which can lead to devastating floods . . .

KLIK!

. . . and harsh droughts.

KLIK!

I need to see the effect of these higher temperatures around the world.

If you want to see how fast things are changing, you should look at glaciers.

RECORD HURRICANES

ACCESS GRANTED: MAX AXIOM

The 2005 Atlantic hurricane season set a new record with 27 named hurricanes and tropical storms. Hurricane Katrina devastated New Orleans in August 2005. It was one of the costliest and deadliest storms ever to hit the United States.

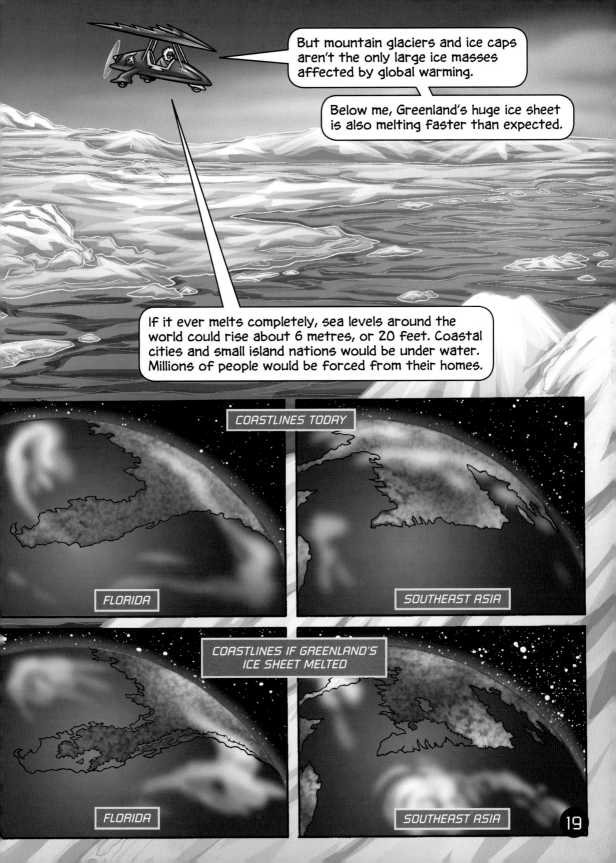

But mountain glaciers and ice caps aren't the only large ice masses affected by global warming.

Below me, Greenland's huge ice sheet is also melting faster than expected.

If it ever melts completely, sea levels around the world could rise about 6 metres, or 20 feet. Coastal cities and small island nations would be under water. Millions of people would be forced from their homes.

COASTLINES TODAY

FLORIDA

SOUTHEAST ASIA

COASTLINES IF GREENLAND'S ICE SHEET MELTED

FLORIDA

SOUTHEAST ASIA

19

But global warming affects more than just humans. It will change animal and plant habitats too.

In fact, many species will have difficulty surviving in the regions where they now live.

Global warming changes habitats faster than plants and animals can adapt.

For instance, polar bears may become extinct if temperatures keep rising. Their hunting grounds are shrinking as the arctic ice melts away.

Global warming is a serious issue, but we can find solutions for our environmental problems.

For example, for many years, gases called chlorofluorocarbons, or CFCs, were used as coolants in freezers and air conditioners.

By the 1980s, scientists had discovered that CFCs were thinning the ozone layer high in the earth's atmosphere.

THINNING OZONE LAYER

Because the ozone layer helps block the sun's harmful ultraviolet rays, people worked together to protect it.

By the 1990s, many countries had agreed to stop using CFCs. Scientists expect the ozone layer to recover around 2065.

SOLAR PANELS

Today, scientists search for solutions to global warming by testing energy sources that don't release greenhouse gases.

For instance, the sun's energy can be captured by solar panels like these.

And wind turbines can generate electricity through wind power.

Engineers are even developing cars powered by cleaner fuels.

In fact, this car's hydrogen engine produces clean water instead of carbon dioxide.

27

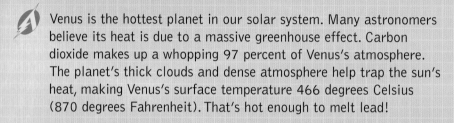

MORE ABOUT GLOBAL WARMING

Venus is the hottest planet in our solar system. Many astronomers believe its heat is due to a massive greenhouse effect. Carbon dioxide makes up a whopping 97 percent of Venus's atmosphere. The planet's thick clouds and dense atmosphere help trap the sun's heat, making Venus's surface temperature 466 degrees Celsius (870 degrees Fahrenheit). That's hot enough to melt lead!

After carbon dioxide, methane is the greenhouse gas most produced by humans. Methane is released by landfills and is a by-product of coal mining. Believe it or not, cows are also a source of methane. When cows burp or pass gas, they release methane. As the demand for beef rises, more cattle are raised and more methane is released into the air.

The United States is responsible for more greenhouse gas pollution than any other country in the world.

Hurricanes have different names depending on where they occur in the world. If they appear on the Pacific Ocean, they're called typhoons. When they form on the Indian Ocean, they're called tropical cyclones.

Ozone gas can be good or bad, depending on where it lies in the atmosphere. The ozone layer 16 to 48 kilometres (10 to 30 miles) high works as a shield to protect life on earth from the sun's dangerous ultraviolet radiation. This radiation can lead to skin cancer in humans. Nearer the earth's surface, ground-level ozone is a health hazard, damaging lungs and hurting plants.

The Arctic's sea ice is also melting quickly. Because snow and ice are white, the sea ice works like a big mirror, reflecting most of the sun's rays. As global temperatures rise, however, some of the polar ice melts. This melting reveals the ocean water below. Because the water is darker than the ice, it absorbs more of the sun's energy and warms up. The warmer water leads to even more of the sea ice melting, which leads to even more water being revealed. The cycle goes on and on.

 You may have seen hybrid cars on the road or on TV. Maybe your family even has one. Hybrid cars run on both petrol and electricity. Because they don't use as much petrol as regular cars, they produce less pollution.

MORE ABOUT

SUPER SCIENTIST

Real name: Maxwell Axiom
Height: 1 m 85 cm (6 ft 1 in.)
Weight: 87 kg (13 st. 10 lb.)
Eyes: Brown   Hair: None

Super capabilities: Super intelligence; able to shrink to the size of an atom; sunglasses give X-ray vision; lab coat allows for travel through time and space.

Origin: Since birth, Max Axiom seemed destined for greatness. His mother, a marine biologist, taught her son about the mysteries of the sea. His father, a nuclear physicist and volunteer park warden, showed Max the wonders of the earth and sky.

One day, while Max was hiking in the wilderness, a megacharged lightning bolt struck him with blinding fury. When he awoke, he discovered a new-found energy and set out to learn as much about science as possible. He travelled the globe studying every aspect of the field. Then he was ready to share his knowledge and new identity with the world. He had become Max Axiom, Super Scientist.

Glossary

atmosphere mixture of gases that surrounds the earth

average common amount of something. An average amount is found by adding figures together and dividing by the number of figures.

carbon dioxide a colourless, odourless gas that people and animals breathe out. Plants need to take in carbon dioxide to live.

climate usual weather that occurs in a place

drought long period of weather with little or no rainfall

fossil fuels natural fuels formed from the remains of plants and animals. Coal, oil, and natural gas are fossil fuels.

glacier huge moving body of ice found in mountain valleys or polar regions

habitat natural place and conditions in which a plant or animal lives

ozone layer thin layer of the gas ozone which is high above the earth's surface. The ozone layer blocks out some of the sun's harmful rays.

photosynthesis the process by which plant cells use energy from the sun to combine carbon dioxide, water, and minerals to make food for plant growth. Photosynthesis releases oxygen into the atmosphere.

radiate give off energy

FIND OUT MORE

Books

Energy Argument: Fossil Fuels, Sarah Irvine (Heinemann Library 2009)

Fuelling the Future series (Heinemann Library, 2008)

No Space to Waste: Population, Yvonne Morrison (Heinemann Library 2009)

On Thin Ice: Climate Change, Lynette Evans (Heinemann Library, 2009)

Pollution Solution?, Sarah Irvine (Heinemann Library, 2009)

Weather (Science Projects series), Joel Rubin (Heinemann Library, 2007)

World in Peril series, Paul Mason (Heinemann Library, 2009)

Websites

http://www.sciencemuseum.org.uk/antenna/climatechange
Check out the pages on the Science Museum website that deal with climate, weather, the greenhouse effect, and who's responsible for climate change.

http://news.bbc/co.uk/cbbcnews
Enter "climate change" in the Search field to find out how this topic has been in the news.

INDEX